The Art of the Deal (er)
An Unauthorized Book on Donald Trump's (Non-Manifest) Principles of Marketing and How They Can Help (or Hurt) Small Businesses and Our Democracy
Adult Coloring Included

Jason McDonald, Ph.D.
https://www.jasonmcdonald.org/
2017 Edition

Copyright © 2017 Excerpti Communications, Inc.

All rights reserved.

ISBN: 1541254910
ISBN 13: 978-1541254916

For Jofus

DISCLAIMER

This book is completely unauthorized and **unendorsed.**
Neither Donald Trump nor anyone on his staff has authorized, endorsed, or participated in the production of this book.

Printed on Recycled Paper in the Republic of Kreplichistan
(Kindle Edition Only)

"I know what you're thinking about," said Tweedledum; "but it isn't so, nohow."
"Contrariwise," continued Tweedledee, "if it was so, it might be; and if it were so, it would be; but as it isn't, it ain't. That's logic."

Lewis Carroll
Through the Looking Glass

Table of Contents
&
Trump's Principles of Marketing

The Art of the Deal(er)   pg. 8

Your Todos -

Teacher, Teach Me…	pg. 10
The No Judgement Zone…	pg. 12
Book Mechanics…	pg. 14
Follow the Trump…	pg. 16
Ce n'est pas un Lapin	pg. 18

Trump's FIRST Principle of Marketing -

#1) Don't Let Reality Confuse You

pg. 20

& His OTHER Principles -

#2) The Internet is Its Own Reality	pg. 22
#3) Use the Internet to Influence the "Real" Reality	pg. 24
#4) Go from the Real to the Social (& Vice-Versa)	pg. 26
#5) Know the Game	pg. 28
#6) Know Your Goal	pg. 30

#7) Project a Clear Brand Image	pg. 32
#8) Be Authentic	pg. 34
#9) Defend Your Brand	pg. 36
#10) Write a Book	pg. 38
#11) Choose Your Networks	pg. 40
#12) Use Twitter (Or Else)	pg. 42
#13) Use the Hashtag	pg. 44
#14) Don't Be Boring	pg. 46
#15) Know Your Target Audience	pg. 48
#16) Ignore Lost Souls	pg. 50
#17) Newsjack the Media	pg. 52
#18) Sow FUD	pg. 54
#19) Emotions Trump Facts	pg. 56
#20) Tell a Story, Not a Statistic	pg. 58
#21) You're Either the Cow, or the Cowboy	pg. 60
#22) Deploy the Non-Factual Counterpunch	pg. 62
#23) Reward Your Fans and Evangelists	pg. 64

THE FUTURE IS UNPREDICTABLE

The Sorcerer's Apprentice	pg. 68
A Trump Marketing Reader	pg. 70
Copyright and Disclaimer Notice	pg. 72

i.
THE ART OF THE DEALER

If you know anything about magic (*which I don't, or perhaps I do*), you'll know that most magic (*except for the real kind*) is based on misdirection (*except when it's based on sorcery*). Especially in cards, when the *dealer* deals.

If you know anything about *marketing*, you'll know that most marketing (*except the honest kind, which doesn't work or perhaps works better than the dishonest kind*) is about *persuasion* and not at all about *reality* (*except that it is really about both, except, of course, when it's more about one than the other*).

And if you've been a citizen (*legal or illegal*) of these United States since November 8, 2016, you may have noticed…

> …that Donald Trump "stole" the election of 2016, if by "stealing," we mean the biggest "political upset" in America in since 1876 … using a lot of Twitter, Facebook, YouTube, Instagram, blog posts, and other **social media marketing** to do it…
>
> … and, **IF** you have enough of an *open mind* to let go of any judgement as to whether Trump is good – or bad – for America, you may have wondered…what can the **Wizard of Marketing**, Donald J. Trump, teach *you* as a *citizen* about what's wrong (*or what's right*) with our democracy, and you as a *businessperson* about how to **build your brand** and **market your business** in the Internet Age, *or how not to?*

That, my friend, is what this book is about.

Adult Coloring Todo. *Find your Crayola colors*, and let's get started. Oh, and how can someone be an *illegal* citizen? No matter.

Coloring Notes and Your Answers To "Is there a difference between real magic and misdirection, real marketing and mismarketing?"

_____
_____
_____
_____
_____
_____
_____
_____

ii.
TEACHER, TEACH ME

Now that Donald Trump is our President, he's clearly too busy to teach. For this reason, this book is a learning manual, a summary, a painful *Common Sense*, an expose, and even an adult coloring book about Trump's **principles of marketing**, especially **social media marketing**. It aims to help *very concerned* citizens understand how he uses marketing for political purposes, and *very concerned businesspeople* grasp Trump's non-manifest (*a very fancy word for invisible*) principles of marketing.

I will be the *Teacher*, and you will be the *Student* (or, contrariwise, Trump will the *Teacher*, and *I* will be the translator). I shall -

- **Summarize** Trump's brand strategy and messaging – the way he builds the Trump brand and aims it at a strategic political audience (conservatives, and the working class, and *not at all at the very serious people in the media* except when he does).
- **Explain** how Trump uses **social media** sites like Twitter, Facebook, Instagram, and YouTube to grow and promote his business / political objectives and personal brand (*in a very serious way, except when he's being facetious*).
- **Give practical advice** to anyone who wants to do the same for a small business, nonprofit, personal brand, or political cause or campaign (*God help you*).
- **Help** *very concerned* citizens understand the genius of Donald J. Trump as a political demagogue or great political leader (*whichever you prefer, or neither, as the case may be*).

Adult Coloring Todo. As you color this *very serious* and perplexed man (*who looks a lot like Paul Krugman*), imagine if you could have a telepathic conversation with Donald Trump on the Principles of Marketing, what would you like to learn?

COLORING NOTES AND YOUR ANSWERS TO "WHAT WOULD YOU LIKE TO LEARN FROM DONALD TRUMP, THE MARKETER?"

_____
_____
_____
_____
_____
_____
_____

iii.
The No Judgement Zone

Is Donald Trump a *threat* to our democracy, or perhaps the *savior* of said democracy? *Do we have a democracy?* For the purposes of this book, it doesn't matter, and I don't care.

Let's get **judgement** out of the way.

> This book isn't about "judging" Donald Trump. Is he good? Is he bad? Is he evil? Is he the Savior, or the Devil? *Is his hair really that color?*

This book isn't about judgement. Rather, this book is about the **HOW**. *How does Trump do what he does?*

It's about the *how* of Trump marketing, the *how* of *how* Donald does what Donald does via social media, and about what you can learn in terms of tips, tricks, and tactics to use Twitter, Facebook, YouTube and other social media networks to understand politics in our democracy, market your own business, bolster your own personal brand, and make sense of Trump, the *political entrepreneur*.

- Along the way we're going to laugh *at* Donald Trump, laugh *with* Donald Trump, and yet *admire* the man for the genius of marketing and politics that he truly is.

Adult Coloring Todo. Color in the cat on the next page and "let go" of your emotions about Trump – *positive* or *negative*. Imagine you're the cat struggling with not judging the mouse he's examining. He may be tempted to just 'kill' and 'eat' the mouse (*sorry vegetarians*), but the cat realizes you can't kill your mouse and have it, too. *So the mouse must live if the cat can learn.* Enter the "No Judgement Zone," so we can observe and learn from Mr. Trump.

COLORING NOTES AND YOUR ANSWERS TO "CAN YOU ENTER THE 'NO JUDGEMENT ZONE' ?"

_____
_____
_____
_____
_____
_____
_____

iv.
BOOK MECHANICS

This book is a *very serious* book about our democracy and a very *not serious* book about marketing (*or the reverse*, I'm not sure which). Each Chapter ends with an "Adult Coloring Todo" – a way to reflect on what you've learned and brainstorm **todos**.

Throughout the book, I use **JMLINKS.com** to reference external web resources. Just visit **http://jmlinks.com/** and enter the referenced "jump code" (*for example*, **22v**) to visit each resource on the Web such as **https://www.donaldjtrump.com/**.

Get Free Stuff

You can get incredible free SEO and Social Media Marketing tools by subscribing to my mailing list at **http://jmlinks.com/free**. Even better, write a short, honest review of this book somewhere on the Internet and get a free copy of one of my workbooks, the *SEO Fitness Workbook* or *Social Media Marketing Workbook*. Use **http://jmlinks.com/contact** or Tel. 800-298-4065 for details.

And Who am I?

My name is **Jason McDonald**, and I teach social media marketing and SEO ("Search Engine Optimization") at Stanford's Continuing Studies Program, at the Bay Area Video Coalition, AcademyX, and for my own company. After Al Gore and I invented the Internet in 1994, I've spent the last twenty three years decoding and deciphering how to market on Google, Bing, Facebook, Twitter, Instagram, YouTube, Snapchat, My Space (*well, not My Space*), and helping "mere mortals" make sense of the New Marketing.

Adult Coloring Todo. You're about to embark on a fun-filled learning adventure. I'll be your guide, so I recommend you color this picture of me and paste it to your refrigerator.

Coloring Notes and Your Answers To "What are the mechanics of this book, and who is this weird guy, Jason McDonald?"

_____
_____
_____
_____
_____
_____
_____

v.
FOLLOW THE TRUMP

It's an open secret that **social media networks** – especially Twitter, Facebook, YouTube and Instagram – have been critical to Trump's political success. Hillary spent millions on traditional advertising, only to be defeated. Trump relied on an Internet-oriented "free media" strategy and won.

To learn from Trump, the deal**ER**, as a master social media marketer, you must "follow him" *at least in social media, if not in real life or politics*. Here's where -

> Twitter - https://twitter.com/realDonaldTrump
>
> Facebook - https://www.facebook.com/DonaldTrump/
>
> YouTube – http://jmlinks.com/21t.
>
> Instagram
> https://www.instagram.com/realdonaldtrump/

Make sure to follow him on SnapChat as well (*realdonaldtrump*) as well as the hashtags #MakeAmericaGreatAgain (Twitter at **http://jmlinks.com/21u**, Instagram at **http://jmlinks.com/21v**) and #MAGA (Twitter at **http://jmlinks.com/21w**, Instagram at **http://jmlinks.com/21x**). For a complete archive of all of Trump's tweets visit **http://jmlinks.com/22d**. Every concerned citizen should follow our **dealER** in Chief on social media, so do it now.

Adult Coloring Todo. Social media is a party, so color in this crazy dog and crazy cat partygoers as you seek *first to understand*, and *second to draw lessons* from Trump on social media to use for your own personal, business, or political parties or marketing. Party on!

COLORING NOTES AND YOUR ANSWERS TO "CAN YOU FIND AND FOLLOW TRUMP AND HIS FOLLOWERS ON SOCIAL MEDIA?"

_____
_____
_____
_____
_____
_____
_____

vi.
Ce N'est Pas un Papin
(This is not a rabbit.)

You've probably gotten very tired of sitting there next to your sister or brother (or boss) watching *CNN*, or reading the *New York Times* and listening to *very serious* people debate *very seriously* whether Donald Trump is good or bad for our democracy, without those same *very serious people* explaining why they didn't see *this* coming, and why we should continue to take them *very seriously* in this New World Order. *I know I have.*

But that's only if you're *against* Trump (which I assume you are) or you're *for* Trump (which I assume you aren't). Or, let me just say I'll assume the *reverse* if the *reverse* makes more sense, but what I'm really trying to do or say is to get you to open your mind to the wit, wisdom and genius of Donald J. Trump.

So as we begin, as you ponder what Trump can and could teach you about marketing (if he had time to write a new book, or the inclination, *whichever comes first*) and what you might learn about marketing from Trump, please begin (*very slowly at first but very rapidly after a while*) to disassociate yourself from the idea that to understand Trump one has to understand *reality* (if by *reality*, you mean the *reality* as *very serious* people like Paul Krugman of the *New York Times* means it). We're going "through the looking glass" to ponder and understand **marketing**, which in the way of Aristotle is much more about **rhetoric** than **reality**. Take a deep breath, and a peek downwards...

And so we begin.

Adult Coloring Todo. You might want to Google, "The Treachery of Images," as the next Chapter is Chapter 1, with Trump's first (and more important) principle of marketing: **don't let reality confuse you**. Which is his first principle of reality as well.

Coloring notes and Your Answers to "Ceci n'est pas un lapin — This is not a Rabbit, or is it?"

_____
_____
_____
_____
_____
_____
_____
_____
_____

The First Principle
Don't Let Reality Confuse You

Trump's first principle of marketing (useful in both politics and in business) is that he **doesn't let reality confuse him**.

Reality is complicated, messy, full of facts and statistics (as well as opposing viewpoints) that *very serious people* use to befuddle, bewitch, confuse and conundrumify the rest of us.

If Donald had let reality confuse him when he declared his candidacy, he would have never *run*. And never *won*.

After all, *very serious people* thought that Hillary Clinton had *gravitas*, Jeb Bush had *money* and a *name*, and Marco Rubio had *better hair*. And *very serious* people thought the flip phones were "just fine," thank you very much, before Steve Jobs gave us the iPhone.

Reality said that Trump couldn't win, but Donald Trump didn't (and doesn't) let *reality* confuse him.

- *Reality* is all about the *present*: what is, what can be measured or counted, statistics and facts.
- Entrepreneurship and marketing (and politics, too), in contrast, are as much about the *future*: what can be, what might be, what you can envision to be.
- Your customers (voters) *don't necessarily know what they want*, because they can't visualize the future that *you're going to create* for them.

Adult Coloring Todo. This girl is looking to the future, and seeing a future in which SHE IS IMPORTANT and HER CUSTOMERS want what she has. As you color her in, imagine what your customers want, *tomorrow*, that they don't necessarily realize they want, *today*.

Coloring notes and Your Answers to "How Reality Confuses You but Shouldn't."

_____
_____
_____
_____
_____
_____
_____
_____
_____
_____

#2
THE INTERNET IS ITS
OWN REALITY

If Donald's first principle of marketing is to "not let reality confuse him," his second is to grasp that the *Internet is its own reality*. Trump was quick to comprehend that there's a "Facebook reality," a "Twitter reality," and even a "Blogosphere reality" or a "TV reality." (*Don't confuse the reality of the Internet, and the reality of Facebook, of Twitter, of YouTube, etc. with the "reality" that you and I inhabit as carbon-based life forms!*)

If Trump has more followers on Twitter than Hillary Clinton (*which he does*), he's more important (*which he is*). Or, take a simple business example like a DUI / DWI attorney. There's DUI attorneys Zhou & Chini (**http://jmlinks.com/21y**) with 1785 likes on Facebook, DUI attorney Macktaz (**http://jmlinks.com/21z**) with 299 likes but 11 reviews, and DUI attorney Jennifer Zide (**http://jmlinks.com/22a**) with 565 likes and 4 reviews. *Which attorney is better?* Well, in the world of Facebook, these attorneys at least know to *play the game of Facebook*, whereas the ones who are not "on" Facebook are invisible and certainly unimportant!

- A person or company or idea or product or service can be **VERY IMPORTANT** on Google or Yelp or Twitter or Facebook or YouTube or Instagram or Snapchat, etc., as judged **BY THAT REALITY**.

Adult Coloring Todo. A cat with 3D glasses and a clapperboard is clearly VERY IMPORTANT in the reality of cats who make movies. If he has his own Facebook Page with many followers, he's important on Facebook as well! As you color him in, open up Facebook, Yelp, Instagram, and ponder what's "real" to your customers on each network. Are you or your business a "cool cat" or a "loser" on each medium?

Coloring Notes and Your Answers to "What is the internet reality for your business or political organization?"

_____
_____
_____
_____
_____
_____
_____
_____
_____
_____

#3
USE THE INTERNET REALITY TO INFLUENCE THE "REAL" REALITY

Here's Trump's third and critical principle of marketing: that the "reality" of the Internet can be used to influence the "reality" inhabited by voters or customers. By Tweeting, Facebooking, Instagramming, and YouTubing, again and again, things like this -

> @realDonaldTrump 1 Oct 2016. Heading to Pennsylvania for a big rally tonight. We will MAKE AMERICA GREAT AGAIN!

Trump's Twitter drove people to his rallies, and that drove the attention of the traditional media, which in turn drove more people to attend his rallies, and follow him on Twitter, Facebook, etc....

Now, let's apply this to the business example of a small pizza restaurant in Enid, Oklahoma (**http://jmlinks.com/21s**). The restaurant with the MOST and BEST online reviews on Yelp or Google or Facebook is the one that people will believe is truly good! And they'll show up "in the real world" to give it a try, giving it the chance to *become and stay* the #1 pizza restaurant in Enid.

- Since the reality on the Internet can influence the reality in the real world, you can and should follow Trump in using the Internet to influence the real reality (and your profits).

Adult Coloring Todo. This Chihuahua loves pizza! Color him – he's adorable, and – if you're nice – he'll write you a review on Facebook, Yelp or Google. Then his friends will see that you sell dog-friendly pizza, and you'll be the #1 pizza restaurant on Yelp for Chihuahuas. If a Chihuahua can like pizza, you can use social media to get more customers or voters!

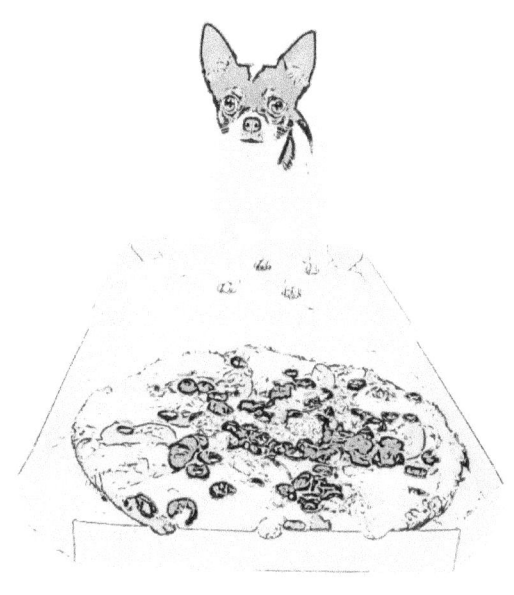

COLORING NOTES AND YOUR ANSWERS TO "HOW CAN YOU USE THE INTERNET REALITY TO INFLUENCE THE 'REAL' REALITY?"

_____
_____
_____
_____
_____
_____
_____

#4
GO FROM THE REAL TO THE SOCIAL
(AND VICE-VERSA)

There's this amazing social network. It's called the "real world!" It can both be supported by, and support, your social media efforts.

Donald Trump understands how the *real* supports the *social*, as well as how the *social* supports the *real*. Take a look at videos from Trump's rallies on YouTube (**http://jmlinks.com/19q**). Watch a few videos, and look at the view counts. One of the most popular videos is when a kid asks Donald Trump what the wall will be made from (**http://jmlinks.com/19r**) at 3.2 million views, 28,000 thumbs up, 18,000 thumbs down, and hundreds of comments.

Trump's rallies appeared on YouTube, and YouTube spurred more attendance at his rallies. The rallies promoted his social media – his Facebook, his Twitter, his YouTube, and social media promoted his rallies.

- Trump encouraged a "virtuous circle" from the *real* to the *social*, and from the *social* back to the *real*.

You can (and should) do this, too. It can be as simple as the cashier at a sporting goods store ASKING customers to follow the store on Facebook, Twitter, and YouTube, and explaining, "Why?" *Because we share videos on how to use those skis you just bought, so you don't look like an idiot – that's why.* Or coupons and insider deals.

Adult Coloring Todo. Imagine you're in the real world talking to a real customer. Not tweeting to one, not Snapchatting to one. But actually talking with one. How will you motivate her to follow you on Facebook, Twitter, Instagram, YouTube or Snapchat? *What's in it for her, not you?*

COLORING NOTES AND YOUR ANSWERS TO "HOW YOU CAN MOTIVATE CUSTOMERS OR VOTERS TO FOLLOW YOU ON SOCIAL MEDIA?"

_____
_____
_____
_____
_____
_____
_____

#5
KNOW THE GAME

What game are we playing? Is it football or soccer, croquet or three-dimensional cheese? Are we having a formal English tea or a frat party? Trump's fifth principle of marketing (and success) is to **know the game**.

For example, despite the complaints of *very serious people* like California Senator Barbara Boxer, the "game" of becoming US President is decided by the Electoral College, not the popular vote, and that "game" is decided very much by swing states like Pennsylvania or Michigan, and not Oklahoma or Oregon.

Now, you can blather on like Senator Boxer, who is introducing *dead-on-arrival* legislation to abolish the Electoral College (**http://jmlinks.com/22w**), or you can know the game and play the game, to win, like Donald Trump did and does. In fact, as an outside observer, you can ask the question of what "game" Senator Boxer is actually playing other than convincing her own ego that she is a *very important person* or her constituents that she's a *very effective Senator*, when in fact she's probably neither.

Or, to turn to a marketing game like SEO (Search Engine Optimization), which is the art of magically appearing at the top of Google, the "game" that's being played isn't about being "best" in the real world but "best" in the eyes of Google. You can complain that Google rules this game, or you can learn the rules to win the game, or both (*but most people do one or the other*).

Adult Coloring Todo. Imagine you're a very sad boxer having a very sad conversation with a very sad California Senator. Amidst tears, you might ask her, "What game does she think she's playing?"

Coloring Notes and Your Answers To "What Game are you playing, and what are the rules by which you win?"

_____
_____
_____
_____
_____
_____
_____
_____

#6
KNOW YOUR GOAL(S)

Donald Trump knows his goals and the order in which they must be achieved:

Goal #1: Become Republican nominee. (*Accomplished!*)

Goal #2: Win the Presidential election (*Accomplished!*)

Goal #3: Be a fantastic President (*Working on this one, now!*)

Goal #4: Open an incredible Presidential Library (*Tbd*).

Whereas Hillary ran against Bernie Sanders "hard enough" to win the nomination but not "so hard" as to alienate his supporters, and looked past the election to the transition, Donald Trump was focused on the goal of each phase, in order. Currently, he's working on the goal of becoming a *very good* President. Critics and naysayers will say that he's going to fail, but Trump would retort that *"That's it's his problem to have, isn't it?"* Compared with the problems of Hillary Clinton, this is a pretty good problem, no?

Similarly in business marketing, the goal of a "cold call" is to get the appointment, not make the sale. And the goal of SEO is to get to the top of Google, not get the sales lead. The goal of a Facebook post is to get the like, and the goal of a YouTube video is to first, get the view, and then get the click. Principle #6 is to know your goals, see them in sequence, and be focused.

Adult Coloring Todo. Clearly defined goals are critical to success in marketing online, whether it's SEO (*get to the top of Google for free*) or social media marketing (*use Facebook, Twitter, etc., to build your brand and spread your business message*). Color in this goalie and ask yourself, what's the goal of the *game* you're playing? How does having a Facebook Page (Twitter account…) assist in that goal?

COLORING NOTES AND YOUR ANSWERS TO "WHAT ARE YOUR GOALS, AND HOW CAN SOCIAL MEDIA AND SEARCH HELP TO ACHIEVE THEM?"

_____
_____
_____
_____
_____
_____
_____
_____

#7
PROJECT A CLEAR BRAND IMAGE

Successful leaders (both business and political) project strong and clear personal brands, both offline and online. Elon Musk, of Tesla, for example, projects a brand image of a can-do technology entrepreneur. Stephen Hawking projects a brand image of a brilliant scientist who has overcome personal adversity. And, Donald Trump follows Principle #7 to be:

- **Brash** – Trump tells it "like it is."

- **Authentic** – he pulls no punches, and you feel that it's really Donald Trump talking not some professional political pundit.

- **Can Do** – he projects a "get it done," "no nonsense" attitude.

- **Alpha Male** – Donald's #1, he's "great" and if you tangle with him, you can expect him to pull no punches.

A strong brand means that you know who you are, what you represent, and <u>so does everyone else</u>. It doesn't necessarily mean you're factual or true, that they like you or agree with you, but it **does** mean that you're **clear.** *Compare Trump's brand to Hillary Clinton's, Jeb Bush's, or Marco Rubio's. Who is clear, and who is a fuzzy fuzz fuzz?*

Adult Coloring Todo. Color this dog, but imagine opening his eyes (and yours) to what your personal / business / product / service brand IS and REPRESENTS for your target customers. If this dog asked you to explain your brand in ten words or less, could you give him a clear answer? If so, write it down. If not… ?

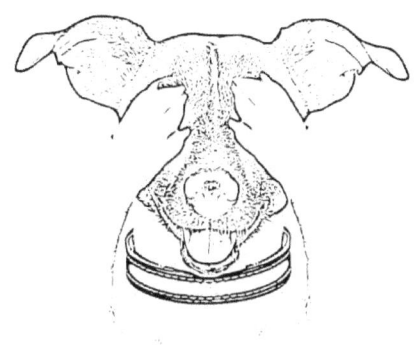

Coloring Notes and Your Answers To "What is your brand image in ten words or less?"

_____
_____
_____
_____
_____
_____
_____
_____
_____
_____

#8
BE AUTHENTIC

Being **authentic** on social media matters more than being slick and professional and as much, if not more, than being truthful. For example, watch Susan Boyle's incredible audition at **http://jmlinks.com/19p** with 202 million (!) views. She almost shames the audience at their prejudice and into amazement at her God-given talent. (*I cry every time I watch it*).

Trump is authentic, while Obama or Clinton often aren't. Take a look, for example, at the difference between the Twitter accounts of Hillary Clinton, and Donald Trump. On Clinton's you'll see:

> *@HillaryClinton* **Tweets from Hillary signed –H.**

Meaning it's not always Hillary who's Tweeting – it's some robotic staff member. *But who wants to listen to the tweets of a Hillary staffer?* **NO ONE.** Not so on @realDonaldTrump. All tweets are his alone, so when you read –

> *@realDonaldTrump Dec 10 As a show of support for our Armed Forces, I will be going to The Army-Navy Game today. Looking forward to it, should be fun!*

You know you're reading Trump's tweets, including his angry tweets. Hilary and Obama made fun of him during the campaign for tweeting "with no filter," but who's laughing now?

Adult Coloring Todo. Color this wise, soulful owl and imagine it's the authentic and wise you. The *you* you are when you sing in the shower, the *you* your company is when you produce incredible products or services, the *you* when you're a politician who truly cares. Be **authentic** on social media to be successful: Principle #8.

COLORING NOTES AND YOUR ANSWERS TO "HOW CAN YOU BE AUTHENTIC ON TWITTER, FACEBOOK, INSTAGRAM, YOUTUBE…?"

_____
_____
_____
_____
_____
_____
_____
_____

#9
DEFEND YOUR BRAND

Is Donald Trump a cyber bully? It's hard to see how Trump can simply ignore criticisms without appearing to be a phony. By responding quickly and fiercely, Trump sends a signal of strength and makes it costly and dangerous to challenge him online!

Among the most famous Trump battles was between Trump and Fox news host Megyn Kelly (**http://jmlinks.com/19u**). In a nutshell, Kelly asked Trump hard questions about his attitudes towards women, and Trump fired back on Twitter that Kelly was having "female problems." Trump has attacked other journalists such as Jeff Zeleny of CNN over voter fraud allegations, and hasn't hesitated to talk tough against China, which complained after Trump spoke with Taiwan's Tsai Ing-wen in violation of the long-standing "one China" policy.

What this means for you is a) monitor your company's or political boss's reputation online, and b) defend that reputation if attacked. You work hard to define a strong, positive brand online, so you must take steps to defend it! **Principle #9 is to defend your brand.** This can be as simple as working to keep customers happy and forestall negativity, responding to negative reviews on Yelp or GlassDoor.com, kicking negative fans off your Facebook page, or even litigating against competitors and customers that post false or defamatory content online. Trump realizes how important his reputation is (*Note: he's perceived as <u>tough</u>, not necessarily as <u>truthful</u>, so he defends the toughness part! Food for thought, no?*).

Adult Coloring Todo. The best defense is often a good offense. Color in T-Rex – king of the dinosaurs - and imagine yourself a fierce defender of your company's reputation online. Roar! When you finish, especially if you're a politician, ponder how T-Rex went extinct and was superseded by meek mammals about the size of a mouse after an asteroid hit Mexico.

Coloring Notes and Your Answers To "Who wants to hurt your brand, and how can you defend against them?"

_____
_____
_____
_____
_____
_____
_____

#10
WRITE A BOOK

Very serious people write books, and *very smart* people realize that *anyone* can write a book. The rest of us think that someone who publishes a book *must be smart*. Trump knows this and has authored many books over the years, from his classic *The Art of the Deal* to *Great Again* to *Think Big* to *Never Give Up* and so on and so forth.

His Amazon author bio (**http://jmlinks.com/21e**) positions him as a "thought leader:"

> *An accomplished author, Mr. Trump has authored over fifteen bestsellers and his first book, The Art of the Deal, is considered a business classic and one of the most successful business books of all time. Mr. Trump has over eight million followers on social media and is a frequent guest across a variety of media platforms.*

Amazon has made it easy to self-publish eBooks and books with its CreateSpace, Kindle Direct, and ACX platforms (**http://jmlinks.com/22x**). If you don't want to go the route of Amazon, you can create a PDF eBook of *frequently asked questions* (for instance) to host on your own website. You can then share it on social media as a free download to capture email addresses.

- Writing a book makes you smart and sexy and a "thought leader."

Adult Coloring Todo. Can cats or dogs read? Humans do, and your really motivated prospects may be keen on an eBook or book that answers their questions. *Write a short book, and become a thought leader in your industry.* But first color in this cat!

Coloring Notes and Your Answers To "Should you write a book or eBook and if so, about what?"

_____
_____
_____
_____
_____
_____
_____

#11
CHOOSE YOUR NETWORKS

Quick, what is Donald Trump's favorite social media network? **Twitter**! Why? Well, it's not just because it's because Trump might believe that everything that really matters in life can be expressed in less than 140 characters. No, it's because Twitter is "Where it's at" politically – news and politics are on Twitter, which is why you use @ signs on Twitter (*because it's where it's @*).

After Twitter, Trump is on Facebook, and after that on YouTube and Instagram. Donald *fishes where the fish are*, and the voters are on Twitter, Facebook, Instagram, and YouTube. A few of them are on SnapChat, so Trump is occasionally on SnapChat, but most of the ones on SnapChat are only thirteen so their voter participation rate is very low (*unless they're illegal, in which case they apparently participate in a LOT of fraudulent voting*).

The point is Trump is NOT on LinkedIn, because LinkedIn is the *serious business* network, not the *political* network. And he's not on Google+ because no one uses Google+, not even Googlers. He's strategic: he researched which ones "made sense" to be President and he worked very, very hard at being good at those and ignored the others.

Your **todo**, therefore, is to survey the Internet universe and decide which network(s) make the most sense. Identify the networks that make the most sense for your business or political organization (and work HARD on those). Principle #11 of "Choose your networks" means use the ones that your customers use.

Adult Coloring Todo. Do you LIKE to be focused? Do you LIKE to achieve a high ROI? Well, if so, as you color in this stylized "like," recall the origin of what Thumbs Up meant in Rome (OK, you can Google it), and think about which social media networks are where "your fish" are.

Coloring Notes and Your Answers To "Which social networks have your target customers or audiences?"

_____
_____
_____
_____
_____
_____
_____

#12
USE TWITTER OR ELSE

Donald Trump **seriously** loves Twitter! In fact, Trump told Lesley Stahl of *Sixty Minutes* that Twitter is a "modern form of communication" and that Twitter "should be nothing that you're ashamed of… it's where it's at" (**http://jmlinks.com/21r**). He explained that social media was more important than paid ads, and that social media was one of the reasons he won the election!

Our President loves Twitter! (And he loves Facebook, YouTube, and Instagram). So what are you waiting for, here's Principle #12 of Marketing: **use Twitter (or else)**, meaning dive right in, starting doing AND learning (at the same time).

You might conclude Twitter is NOT where your customers hang out; if so, identify and use the ones they DO use. The point is to "get serious" about social media. Trump didn't wait till he had a perfect understanding of Twitter, of what's a hashtag and what's a handle, or what's a retweet or what's a DM. Once he realized Twitter was "where it's at" for him as a politician, he dove in both feet first. He's a doer and not a thinker: he's unafraid, and he just started doing Twitter.

- If Trump teaches us nothing else, he teaches us that you should recognize an opportunity and dive right in. Go big and go bold!

Adult Coloring Todo. Look closely. This man is chasing birds that are actually dollar bills. That's what Twitter is: a bird that can make you money. (*Or Yelp can, or Facebook can, or Google can*). Think of all the money you can make as you color in the dollar bills, and then stop coloring and start Tweeting! Or Facebooking or Yelping or YouTubing or Google Plussing (*OK, not Google+*).

Coloring Notes and Your Answers To "How can you stop being afraid, and just start 'Doing' Twitter (or Facebook, etc.)?"

_____
_____
_____
_____
_____
_____
_____
_____
_____

# #
USE THE HASHTAG

Hashtags exist on nearly every social network, but especially on Twitter and Instagram (and to a lesser extent on Facebook). A hashtag is a **conversation**. For example, the hashtag #MakeAmericaGreatAgain (**http://jmlinks.com/19w**) or #MAGA (**http://jmlinks.com/21w**) is a way for Trump's fans, followers and even critics to have a conversation on Twitter about his campaign. Anyone can "chime in," no holds barred.

Other Trump hashtags are #DraintheSwamp, #NeverHillary, and #TrumpTrain.

Trump uses hashtags in two ways –

1. To chime in on an existing conversation (one he didn't start or originate, like #GOP or #Debate2016).
2. To create a new conversation around which his followers can interact like #TrumpTrain or #ThankYouTour2016.

Like Trump, you can use hashtags in two ways. First, to piggyback on existing conversations such as #losangeles (the conversation about Los Angeles) or you can create your own such as #JasonMcDonaldspizza (if you were a pizza restaurant). Read more about hashtags at the official Twitter explanation at **http://jmlinks.com/19x**. Think of a hashtag as an open conversation on Twitter, Instagram or Facebook (*anyone – and I do mean anyone – can chime in*), and you've grasped the concept.

Adult Coloring Todo. Enjoy these colorful clowns having a conversation, and investigate which online conversations by your customers or potential customers might make sense for your brand, business, or nonprofit. Hashtag: #*Participate* #Itsfun.

Coloring Notes and Your Answers To "What's a Hashtag, and How Can You Use Hashtags in Business or Politics?"

_____
_____
_____
_____
_____
_____
_____
_____

#14
DON'T BE BORING

Trump tweets with drama, with flair, with authenticity, with a kind of flame-throwing attitude towards online buzz that embraces controversy and provocation.

For example:

> *@realDonaldTrump* Nov 4, 2016 *'ICE OFFICERS WARN HILLARY IMMIGRATION PLAN WILL UNLEASH GANGS, CARTELS & DRUG VIOLENCE NATIONWIDE'*

Anything but boring! Trump uses exclamation points (!) and ALL CAPS. He runs INTO controversy, not away from it! By following Principle #14, *not being boring*, Trump stays top of mind, people engage with and share his message, and the mainstream media often follows along like docile lemmings.

- Can you Tweet like Trump? That is, *not be boring*? Trump gets the fact that there's no point in using Twitter (or Facebook or YouTube) if no one cares. *Do you?*

Yes, it can be a little dangerous, *yes* it might play loose with the facts, but what Trump is teaching us is to **not be boring**.

Adult Coloring Todo. Your customers or voters don't care about you, especially if you don't communicate what you have (*that they want*) and *you're boring*. No one participates in Twitter, Facebook, YouTube, Instagram, etc., to be bored. Watch "Kid President" first at **http://jmlinks.com/5j**, and then color this chipmunk (*he's doing penance for being boring*), and fill in how he's going to NOT BE BORING on social media and neither are you.

Coloring Notes and Your Answers To "How can you be " not boring" – on social media?"

_____
_____
_____
_____
_____
_____
_____
_____

#15
KNOW YOUR TARGET AUDIENCE

Donald Trump knows who his people are: Republicans, conservatives, white America, and especially the working class people who feel like America is not working for them.

Like Moses, Trump didn't come to lead *all* people to the promised land, but rather to lead *his own* people there, first and foremost. Whether intellectually or instinctively, Trump knew (and knows) that working class voters in key swing states like Michigan and Pennsylvania were "his people," and he spoke to his people.

(Compare this with Hillary Clinton who tried to be all things to all people, and ended up being not-that-motivating to not-that-many people). Trump, in contrast, understood his people, and his messaging on Twitter, Facebook, Instagram, and YouTube catered to their hopes, needs, and desires. A sharply defined brand message and a sharply defined target audience constituted Trump's dual formula for success.

Your business or your personal brand can't be all things to all people, and it shouldn't try! McDonald's, for example, aims to service budget-conscious consumers who want quick, cheap burgers, not affluent consumers who want organic quality. And Singapore Airlines, for instance, aims to service luxury-conscious business flyers on long flights to Asia, not those seeking the cheapest fares. Ditto for you and your business or political cause on social media: define your target audience, and focus on THEIR needs.!

Adult Coloring Todo. Good – no great – marketing is all about focus. About knowing who YOU ARE, what YOU HAVE, and WHO WANTS WHAT YOU HAVE. It's being Moses to the Jews, the Beatles to teenage girls in the 1960s, and Donald Trump to America's forgotten working class in 2016. As you color in this dog-as-target, imagine how strong-of-purpose you must be to aim at the apple, hit the apple, you amazingly focused marketer!

Coloring Notes and Your Answers To "Who is your target audience, and what do they want (that you have)?"

_____
_____
_____
_____
_____
_____
_____
_____

#16
IGNORE LOST SOULS

If Donald Trump knows his target audience is, and matches "what he has" with "what they want," he also knows who his target audience is NOT. Trump sees liberal, multicultural America – especially the Media Elite and the establishments of the Democratic party as "lost souls."

He doesn't like them, he doesn't respect them, he doesn't try to win them over, and – when it serves his purpose – he's willing to throw them under the bus to provide amusement to his followers in front of the cameras of social media. Watch, for example, a *New York Times* video of a Trump rally at **http://jmlinks.com/21p** and be appalled or amused at how Trump treats the media.

Trump has taken to calling the *New York Times* the "failing" New York Times on Twitter just as he called Hillary "Crooked Hillary" and Ted Cruz "Lyin' Ted Cruz." As a good marketer, Trump knows who he wants to win over, and who he doesn't or can't win, and he's willing to *use the latter* to *please the former*.

You may not want to be quite this aggressive, but the point is to know who your customers or voters are, and who you will NEVER win over, and stop worrying so much about "lost souls."

- In the immortal words of Taylor Swift, "Haters gotta hate" or from the movie, *The Interview*, "They hate us because they ain't us" (**http://jmlinks.com/22j**).

Adult Coloring Todo. Think for a moment about what group(s) of non-customers you will NEVER win over? Color in this bus-driving dog, and imagine how you can at least "not care" about your haters or, even better, throw them under the bus in a spectacular self-serving way that grabs the attention of your true target customers. Your Snapchat story is waiting to be filmed.

Coloring Notes and Your Answers To "Who is a 'lost soul' to you and can you use them in any way?"

_____
_____
_____
_____
_____
_____
_____

#17
NEWSJACK THE MEDIA

Social media marketing guru, David Meerman Scott coined the term "newjacking" to refer to identifying a trending topic in the news and on social media and "hijacking" that publicity for your own purposes (**http://jmlinks.com/19t**). "Newsjacking" is one of Trump's most effective principles of marketing at #17.

For example, Trump took anxiety over immigration and hijacked that anxiety into chants to "Build the Wall" which created incredible free publicity for Trump over and above any serious discussion of immigration reform. Or during the debates he took serious discussions and hijacked them into discussions about the size of his hands, or whether Marco Rubio sweated too much and other hilarious and disrespectful things. Or when Jill Stein requested a recount, and Trump tweeted that he would have won except for "millions" in votes by illegal immigrants. In fact, Saturday Night Live has so noticed how Trump tweets incessantly to "distract" the media from things he might not want to talk about that it became one of their funniest spoof videos (**http://jmlinks.com/19u**).

- If there's a trending conversation going on in your industry, newsjack it to your brand, product or service. Change the subject, or – if possible – change it to be "all about you."

Adult Coloring Todo. Pirates board other vessels, loot them, and often take them over to sail them to "their" destinations rather than the captain's. Color in this cyber pirate, and brainstorm how you can "be a pirate" vis-à-vis your industry's media and blogs. What trending topics can you newsjack, and how? Aye aye, matey!

Coloring Notes and Your Answers To "What can you 'newsjack' in your industry and how?"

_____
_____
_____
_____
_____
_____
_____
_____

#18
SOW FUD (FEAR, UNCERTAINTY, DOUBT)

Sowing FUD (*fear, uncertainty,* and *doubt*) is a time-proven strategy when up against a fierce competitor. While Hillary Clinton sought to portray Trump as mentally unstable ("Can you trust him with the nuclear codes?"), Trump portrayed Hillary as untrustworthy ("Can you trust her with email?"). IBM famously used FUD against competitor Amdahl, as did Microsoft against its own technology competitors (**http://jmlinks.com/22b**).

When it comes to major issues such as climate change, Trump has used FUD against the overwhelming majority of scientists who believe it is real and caused by human activity. For example -

> @realDonaldTrump 6 Nov 2012 *The concept of global warming was created by and for the Chinese in order to make U.S. manufacturing non-competitive.*

(You can read an archive on Trump's tweets on what he sees as the *global warming hoax* at **http://jmlinks.com/22c**). The principle here is that, if you are facing strong competition or strong idea, sometimes the best response is to sow FUD, and social media is excellent soil for *fear, uncertainty,* and *doubt*. Climate change science, meet FUD.

Adult Coloring Todo. To sow a seed doesn't mean it will germinate. And it might be a weed! Farmer dog is contemplating sowing FUD, but while he might admire Trump for using it, he's not sure he wants to sow FUD as it might be a DUD. Color him in and ask yourself whether FUD is something you might want to use, or just keep in your back pocket as a concept in your marketing.

Coloring Notes and Your Answers To "Would you, could you, should you sow FUD in your market?"

_____
_____
_____
_____
_____
_____
_____
_____

#19
EMOTIONS TRUMP FACTS

Sadly, many marketers overfocus on the *factual* aspect of marketing – the facts and figures, the features and benefits. The really great marketers, however, understand that *emotions* – not facts and figures – *sell* products and services (and Presidential candidates).

What emotion was Donald Trump selling during the 2016 campaign? **Anger!** Anger at politicians who had ruined America. Anger at a "Media Elite" that has failed to tell the truth. Anger at illegal immigrants. Anger at the Republican and Democratic establishments.

And what *emotion* was Hillary selling? If there was one at all, it was perhaps *fear* (of Trump), but more than emotion, she worked on facts, figures, and twelve-point plans. *Boring! Loser!*

Emotions trump facts (pun intended) on Facebook, on Twitter, on YouTube and everywhere in marketing and on social media (except perhaps LinkedIn). Businesses that leverage emotions outdo businesses that stick to (boring) facts. Take a look at the videos on the BlendTec YouTube channel (**http://jmlinks.com/22f**), for example, and notice how few interactions the "serious" videos have compared to the "funny" videos. The most popular video is "Will it Blend? iPad" (**http://jmlinks.com/22g**) which is a super funny video in which they "blend" an iPad.

- Principle #19 - Emotions trump facts. It's a big one.

Adult Coloring Todo. If someone asked you to identify an emotion that signified your business, what would it be? Outrage? Fear? Pathos? Logic? (*Oh, snap – logic isn't an emotion*). Color in this angry cat, but wonder if it is truly angry, fearful, or perhaps laughing? Which emotion will work better for you?

Coloring Notes and Your Answers To "How do emotions trump facts (in your industry)?"

_____
_____
_____
_____
_____
_____
_____
_____

#20
TELL A STORY, NOT A STATISTIC

Hillary Clinton, like all policy wonks, loves facts and statistics. *Boring*!

- Trump's Principle #20, in contrast, is the power of a *story* not a *statistic*.

When Trump "saved" jobs at Carrier in Indiana, he garnered incredible pickup across the news media and pollsters reported an immediate boost in Trump's popularity (**http://jmlinks.com/19y**). While *very serious* economists, statisticians, and even Republicans criticized the deal as more smoke than substance, it didn't really matter. The story trumped the statistics! In fact, Trump's triumph in 2016 is, if you think about it, a narrative. He's telling us a "story" of him as a successful businessman that will morph in to the "story" of him as a successful President.

Turning to social media, take a moment to watch a video like "Dear Future Mom" (**http://jmlinks.com/22e**) which tells a story about Down's Syndrome and pregnancy as opposed to giving statistics. *Would you care about it if it were a scientific study?*

Adult Coloring Todo. Can your business, nonprofit, or political organization tell a story rather than a statistic? Convey an emotion rather than force feed an audience with facts? This cat accountant is trying to convince these two birds to use his services using computer statistics, but might we suggest a story instead? "Once upon a time, there was a hungry accountant…"

Coloring Notes and Your Answers To "How can you tell a story rather than a statistic?"

_____
_____
_____
_____
_____
_____
_____
_____

#21
YOU'RE EITHER THE COW OR THE COWBOY

People use decision shortcuts. *Very serious* author, Daniel Kahneman explains this in his 2011 book, *Thinking Fast and Slow* – with *fast* being using an emotional shortcut route, and *slow* being a smarty pants logical route. Smart marketers focus a lot on brand identity, built on short, simple, often emotional "decision shortcuts" that get associated with a brand. An Apple iPhone is… *easy-to-use, sleek, stylish, powerful*. A BMW is the *ultimate driving machine*, and a McDonald's hamburger is *cheap* and *fast*. A brand is a decision shortcut that a marketer has wormed into our heads.

Trump understands the power of worming his brand and that of his opponents into our psychology, and so during the campaign he branded his opponents, and repeated his brand for them, over and over. Who didn't remember, "Lyin' Ted Cruis," "Little Marco," or "Crooked Hillary?" By repeating the label over and over again, Trump "branded" them as dishonest idiots, and they were unable to overcome his marketing prowess. In contrast, he branded himself as *successful businessman, Alpha male*, and the *man with big hands*.

Remember that the term "branding" comes from the hot iron that was once seared onto a cow's behind to show ownership.

- Blackjack Principle #21 - In marketing, as in politics, it's *brand* or *be branded*.

Adult Coloring Todo. You're either the *cow* or the *cowboy*. So figure out a short, preferably emotional brand for your company and its products or services, and if you're aggressive, think of a few key terms to brand your competitors. *Yee-haw!*

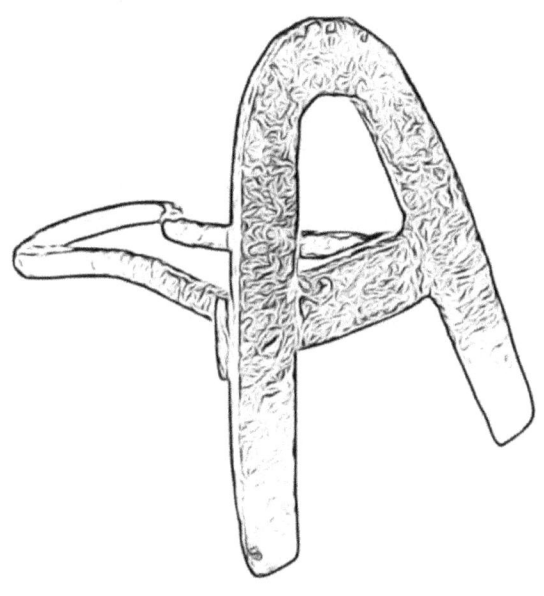

Coloring Notes and Your Answers To "How can you 'brand' and not 'be branded'?"

_____
_____
_____
_____
_____
_____
_____

#22
DEPLOY THE NON-FACTUAL COUNTERPUNCH

Did Hillary Clinton win the popular vote? Most reasonable people would answer yes; most reasonable people would accept the polling numbers as provided by the Registrars of the states. But when Green Party candidate Jill Stein initiated a recount in Michigan, Wisconsin, and Pennsylvania, Trump responded with what I call the "non-factual counterpunch:"

> *@realDonaldTrump 27 Nov 2016 In addition to winning the Electoral College in a landslide, I won the popular vote if you deduct the millions of people who voted illegally*

Despite the fact that there is essentially zero factual evidence for voter fraud on anything remotely approaching this scale, Trump used this tactic to turn the media discussion around. In what some analysts call a "false equivalency," Stein's allegations of voter problems (admittedly skimpy) were juxtapositioned next to Trump's allocation of massive voter fraud (admittedly nearly zero).

Terms like Stephen Colbert's Truthiness (**http://jmlinks.com/21d**), false balance, or the word "post-truth" or "post-factual politics" capture some of this dynamic as well.

- #22 - Sometimes your best strategy is a non-factual counterpunch as a way to "muddy the waters."

Adult Coloring Todo. The best defense can be often a good offense. Since we don't let reality confuse us, sometimes a half truth or even a lie can be a solid marketing strategy. Ethics, anyone? Is this boxer attacking or defending, or perhaps faking?

Coloring Notes and Your Answers To "Who's punching you, and how can you counterpunch them with non-facts?"

_____
_____
_____
_____
_____
_____
_____

#23
REWARD YOUR FANS & EVANGELISTS

A *fan* or *evangelist* on social media is someone who so loves you and your brand that he will "go to bat for you." This could be a positive review on Yelp, a comment or share of a Facebook post, interaction with your hashtags on Instagram or Twitter, of even – in a more aggressive way – "trolling" others on the Internet to ardently defend your brand against detractors.

Trump rewards his fans – Principle #23. One way is by singling them out with retweets on Twitter, for example:

> @realDonaldTrump Dec 17, 2016 "@EazyMF_E: @realDonaldTrump Many people are now saying you will be an extremely successful president! #MakeAmericaGreatAgain" Thank you!

Can you imagine how thrilled *@EazyMF_E* was to be retweeted by the President-elect? And how that motivated other Trump fans to retweet Trump on the chance that they, too, might be so honored? Watch a video of Trump engaging with a little boy fan about what the wall will be made of at **http://jmlinks.com/22h**, and watch this SNL video on Trump retweeting his fans (**http://jmlinks.com/19u**) to see how art imitates life.

- It's *social* media, so do everything you can to honor, motivate, and reward your online fans and evangelists.

Adult Coloring Todo. What makes your fans feel important and special? Imagine your fans filling up a sports stadium cheering for your company. Then, you call out: COME ON DOWN and reward one. How do you do it? How does this motivate the others?

Coloring Notes and Your Answers To "Who are your fans and evangelists, and how can you reward them online?"

_____
_____
_____
_____
_____
_____
_____
_____

THIS PAGE UNINTENTIONALLY LEFT NOT BLANK

Want free stuff?

Visit **http://jmlinks.com/free**
Even better – write a review of this book and get a free copy of the *SEO Fitness Workbook* or *Social Media Marketing Workbook*. Contact me at **http://jmlinks.com/contact** for details.

EPILOGUE

"It's tough to make predictions, especially about the future."

~ Yogi Berra

vii.
THE SORCERER'S APPRENTICE

In Disney's classic 1940 movie, Fantasia, Mickey Mouse is cast as a "sorcerer's apprentice" who exploits the magic of his master wizard, only to unleash it and create a catastrophe (watch it at **http://jmlinks.com/21f**).

Like Mickey Mouse, Donald Trump seems to have unleashed the wizardry of social media marketing to his (temporary?) advantage. Will Trump prove a genius or a fool?

It's too early to tell, of course, but here more than a few scenarios that might come back to bite Trump, among them:

> **Revenge of Reality.** In the short run, one can "ignore" reality, but in the long run (*even on the Internet*) reality has a way of catching up. *Climate change, or Russian aggression, anyone?*
>
> **The Power of Anecdote.** Trump has chosen battles even with ordinary citizens, be they parents of war heroes or union management, but just one anecdote that goes terribly wrong could be a *viral social media catastrophe* to his brand.
>
> **Death by a Thousand Tweets**. The Internet has the power to "crowdsource" information, and – over time – Trump might find that he can't control the Twittersphere, which may begin to believe that the Emperor has no clothes.

Or, he could succeed and be an **incredible President**. That could happen, too. *Really*, it could!

Adult Coloring Todo. "Trump – so far - has proven a worthy teacher and social media marketer, so stay tuned to see whether this Sorcerer's Apprentice will prove the *Wizard*, or only *The Apprentice*, of the magic of social media and the Internet.

Coloring Notes and Your Answers To "What do you think will be the future of Trump, the 'Wizard of Marketing'?"

_____
_____
_____
_____
_____
_____
_____

vii.
A Trump Marketing Reader

If you've read this far, I'll assume you're already following Trump on social media, everything from his Twitter account to his YouTube channel. After he's taken office, be sure to also follow him on all the official channels of the US Government such as the official President Twitter account, **https://twitter.com/potus**.

Be sure to buy and read his classic, *The Art of the Deal* (**http://jmlinks.com/22k**) which is really the best statement of his philosophy as a marketer. There are also a few good articles online that discuss Donald Trump and marketing:

> *The Ingenious Marketing Strategies Behind Trump's Success* (**http://jmlinks.com/22t**).
>
> *Marketing in the Age of Trump* (**http://jmlinks.com/22m**).
>
> *5 Marketing Lessons Learned Watching Donald Trump Run for President* (**http://jmlinks.com/22p**).
>
> *How Marketing Helped Donald Trump Win the 2016 Election* (**http://jmlinks.com/22q**).
>
> *12 Things I learned about Marketing from Donald Trump* (**http://jmlinks.com/22r**).
>
> *6 Lessons from Donald Trump's Winning Marketing Manual* (**http://jmlinks.com/22s**).

You can browse an up-to-date list at **http://jmlinks.com/22u**.

Adult Coloring Todo. You and I are fortunate to live in "interesting times," so remember as you color in the *Cheshire Cat smile* on the next page that the future of Donald Trump and our country, or of you and your marketing is a "blank page" to be filled by him and by you, by me and by everyone. Happy marketing!

Coloring Notes and Your Answers To "What will fill in the 'blank space' of the American future?"

_____
_____
_____
_____
_____
_____
_____

viii.
COPYRIGHT & DISCLAIMER

Copyright © 2017 Excerpti Communications, Inc., All Rights Reserved.

This is a completely unofficial guide to the principles of marketing. Neither Donald Trump nor anyone on his staff or organization has endorsed this book, nor been involved in its production. The same goes for Google, Yahoo, Bing, Facebook, Twitter, Instagram, YouTube, Snapchat and any other social media networks discussed in this book.

- All trademarks are the property of their respective owners. I have no relationship with nor endorsement from the mark holders. Any use of their marks is so I can provide information to you.

Internet marketing changes rapidly, so please be aware that scenarios, facts, and conclusions are subject to change without notice. **Any changes to your Internet marketing strategy is at your own risk.** Neither Jason McDonald nor the JM Internet Group nor Excerpti Communications, Inc. assumes any responsibility for the effect of any changes you may, or may not, make to your website, social media marketing strategy, or advertising based on the information in this book.

www.ingramcontent.com/pod-product-compliance
Lightning Source LLC
Chambersburg PA
CBHW061203180526
45170CB00002B/936